CW01312630

ISBN: 9798690269418

But...

...I don't feel like I have a personal relationship with God

Bible study for young people
who feel that God is distant.

How to use this book

This book is divided into sections:

Prepare - is an opportunity to reflect on your starting point, either individually or in a group discussion.

Bible Study - time to dig deeper into God's word. You will need a Bible handy to complete this section.

Reflection - creative writing to lead you into prayer and reflection.

Going Deeper - offers ideas for personal prayer and reflection.

Ideas for Larger Youth Groups - suggests games, projects and ideas for youth leaders in a large group setting.

Ideas for All Age Worship - suggests ways in which young people could share their learning with God's people of all generations.

Introduction

What do youth workers and Christian leaders actually *mean* when they talk about having a 'personal relationship' with God? Or with Jesus? How can you be in a relationship with someone you've never even seen, or with a God who never seems to speak to you?

There's no denying it - even to seasoned Christians it sometimes feels like God is a long, long way away...

So what is this 'relationship' supposed to look like? How is it supposed to feel? How can you tell if it is there or not?

To these questions there are many right answers, and very few wrong ones. These studies are designed to help you explore what a personal relationship with God looks and feels like *for you*, and to help you find confidence in sharing your thoughts with others.

How to find a Bible Passage

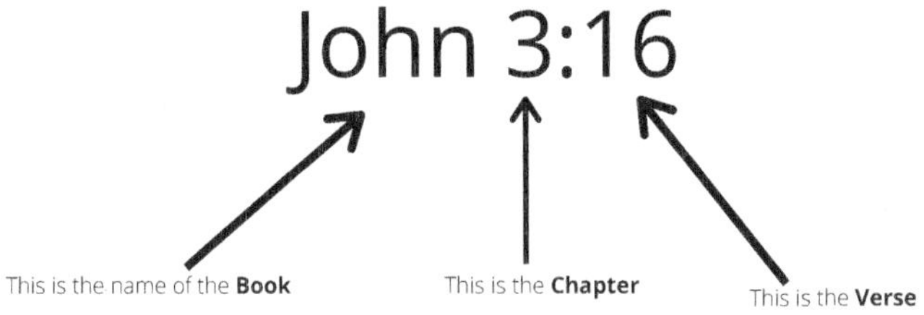

Go to the **Contents** page of your Bible and look up the name of the **book**. (Old Testament and New Testament books might be listed separately, or in alphabetical order instead of page order.)

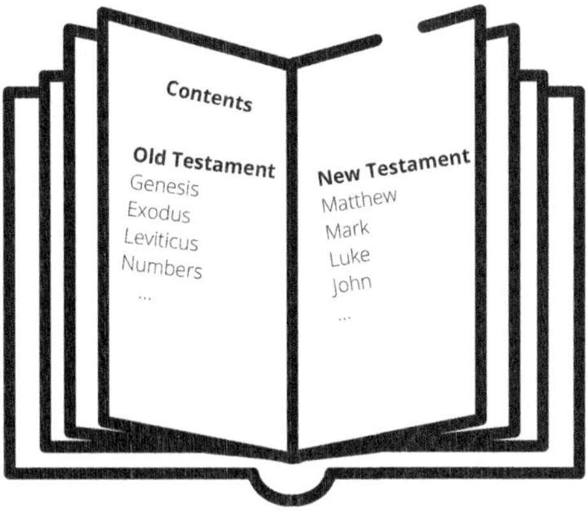

Within each book, the larger numbers at the head of each section are the **chapter** numbers, and the smaller ones within the text are the **verse** numbers.

Prepare

How do you think you would react if Jesus walked into the room right now? (Choose one picture and say why.)

When was the last time you prayed, other than in Church?

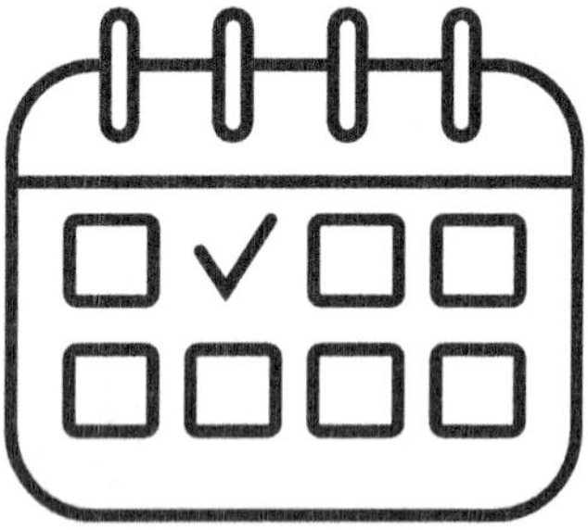

Were you praying for yourself, or someone else?

Think about your closest friend or friendship group. In what ways do you keep in contact with them when you are not together?

Your Thoughts and Reflections.

Use this space to note down your responses to the 'prepare' questions, and any thoughts and feelings as you begin this study book.

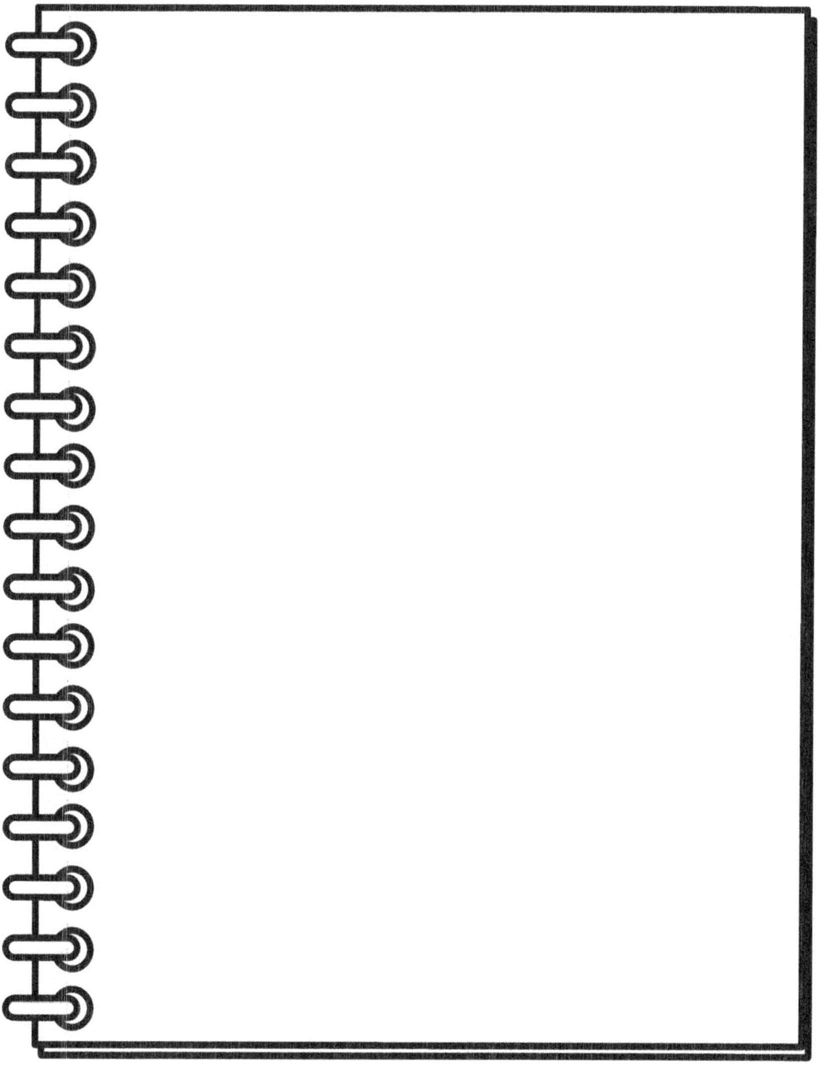

Bible Study 1

But...

...God feels far away.

Who is surprisingly good at knitting?

Psalm 139:1-24

Look again at Psalm 139:13 for the answer.

The Psalms are ancient songs and poems that have been used in worship for centuries. The writers of the Psalms pour out their hearts with raw honesty - which sometimes leads to shocking results! (Turn to Psalm 137:9 to see what I mean, but only if you have a strong stomach!)

At times, this brutal honesty might make us want to squirm, but it also gives us the assurance that we can come before God with whatever we are feeling, whenever we are feeling it.

Psalm 139 is called 'A Psalm of David' - which may mean that it was written *by* King David or it may mean that it was written *for* King David (scholars aren't sure which). In either case, King David was someone whom everybody thought was a man close to God's own heart. (Check out chapter 7 of the book of 2 Samuel to see just how much God favoured King David.)

So, if anyone were to know what a personal relationship with God feels like, then it would be King David - right? Dead right. And David, (or his psalmist - if it wasn't David himself) doesn't keep that wisdom a secret. In Psalm 139 David's relationship with God is laid bare for all to see. So, let's turn there now, and see what we can learn.

Compare Psalm 139:1 with Psalm 139:23. What do you think these two verses tell us about why the Psalmist wrote this piece?

Look at verses 1-6 of the Psalm and make two lists. The first list should be **'What do these veses tell me about God?'** and the second list should be **'What do these verses tell me about myself?'**

Your Notes

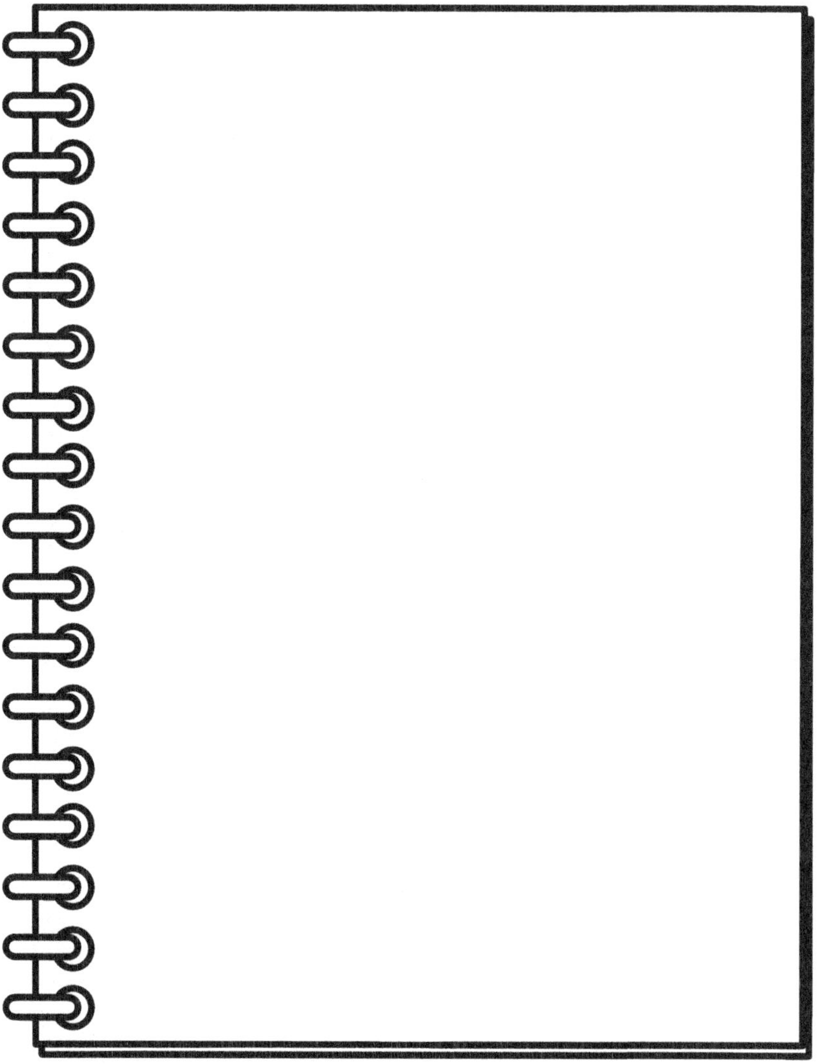

How does it feel to know that God is thinking about you, even when you're not thinking about God?

Have you ever walked through the security scanners at an airport? What does that moment feel like?

In verse 1 the psalmist talks about God searching us, and the word 'know' refers to being known in a complete and absolute way. A bit like those airport scanners - God can see things that other people can't. Is this a comfortable thought?

One thing that can hold us back from a personal relationship with God is sin. In verses 2, 3 and 4 the psalmist reflects on the different ways he might have sinned. How many ways can you identify in these verses?

When you were a little kid and you knew you had done something wrong, did you ever try to hide, or to hide your mistake? It's often what our instincts tell us to do! But what do verses 7-12 tell us about trying to hide from God?

In verse 8 the psalmist speaks of a place called *Sheol*. This was an ancient term for the 'underworld' or realm of the dead.

Rocket = emergency colouring in.

Your Notes

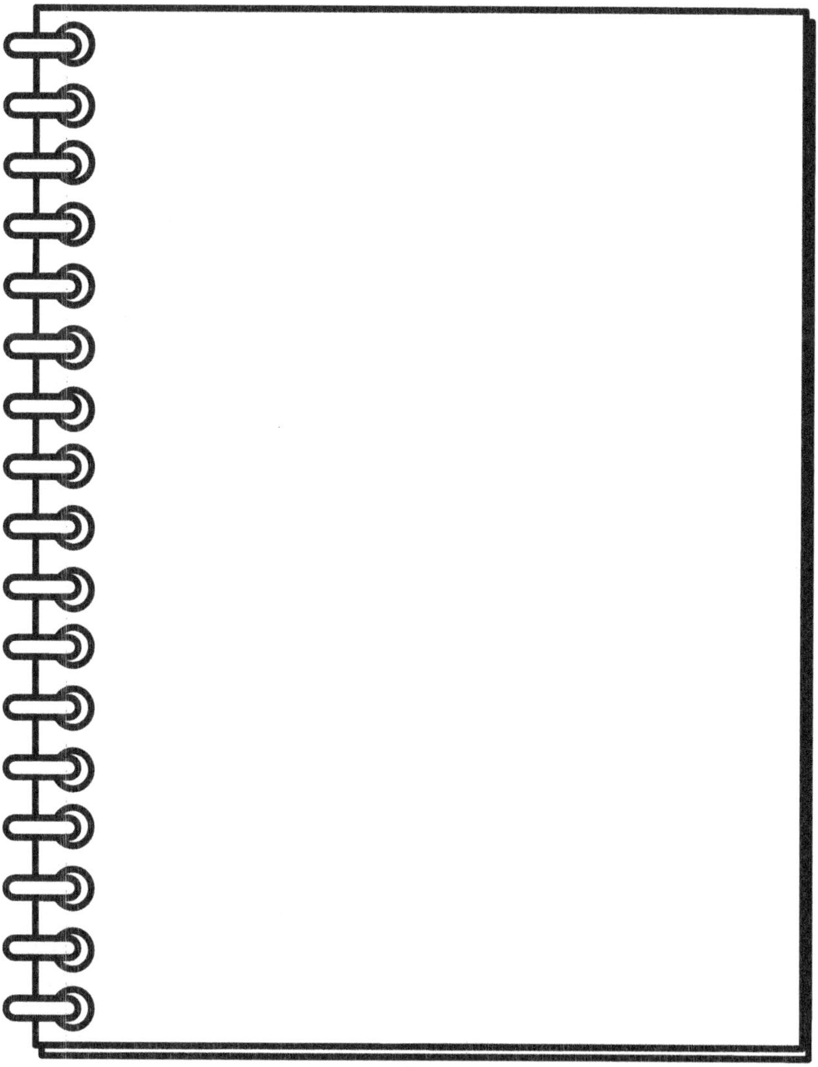

When we realise that we can hide **nothing** and **nowhere** from God, we might be tempted to think that there is **no way** God could love us or want to be in relationship with us! However, just as the psalmist brings us to that point of despair, we get to verse 13 - the centrepiece of Psalm 139.

We're used to the idea that God created our bodies, which form and grow based on what we feed them how much excercise we give them, but have you ever thought about God as the creator of your inward, hidden self? This is the part of you which is your emotions, talents, desires and fears. This too grows based on how it is fed and how it is exercised.

What are some good ways to feed and exercise our inward selves? Look in the following places for some ideas:

Philippians 4:8
2 Timothy 3:16
Proverbs 15:32
Luke 8:14-15
2 Peter1:5-8
Romans 5:3-5

In verses 15 and 16 the psalmist speaks of God knowing him and ordaining the days of his life even before he was in his mother's womb - ('woven in the depths of the earth' refers to the time before the creation of the world).

Of course, Christians hold a range of beliefs when it comes to the creation of the world. But even so, how does it feel to think that God knew you even before the world came into being?

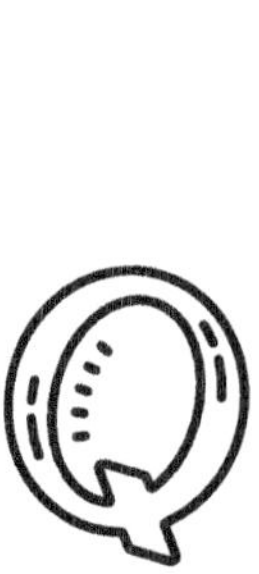

Your Notes

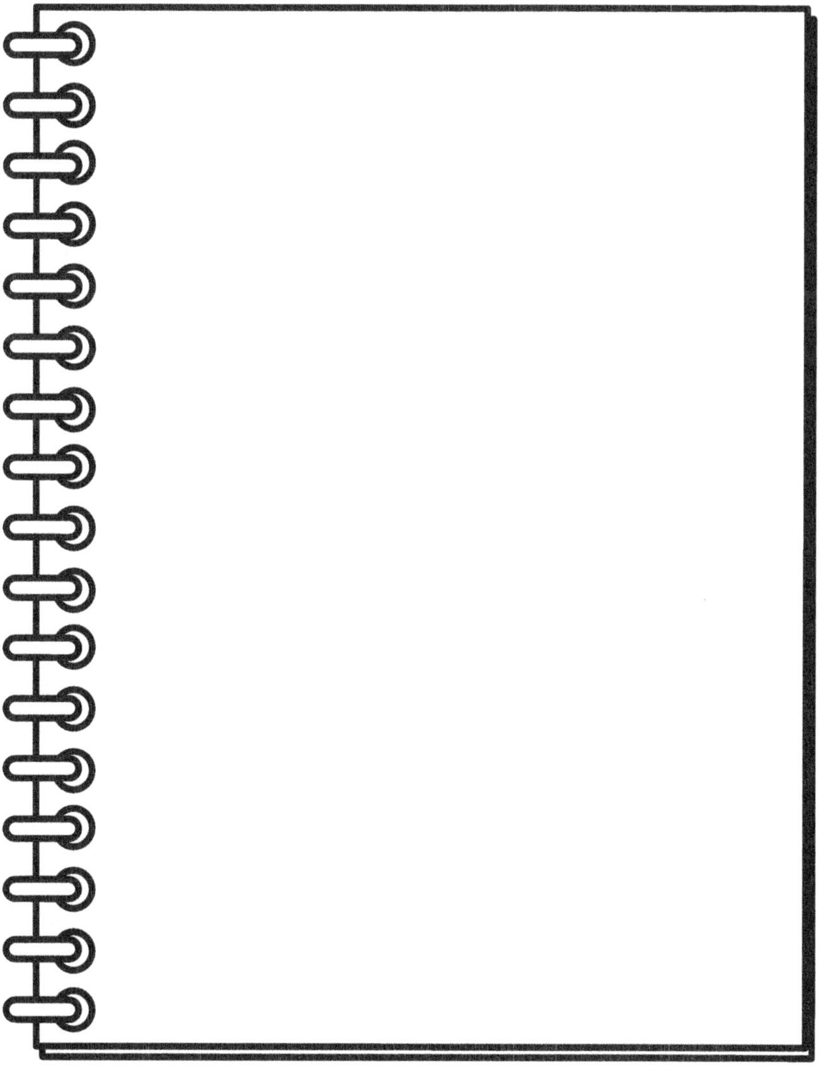

In verses 19-22 the psalmist writes some angry words about those who do not take God seriously. Do you find this surprising? Should the psalmist be 'nicer' about them?

Look closely at what the psalmist says in verse 19. Who is going to be responsible for dealing with the sin of the wicked?

We don't have to pretentd that it is easy to love our enemies, or that we can't see other people's sin. Just like the psalmist, we can take it honestly to God. But we also have to remember that God is judge and we are not. Once we've taken our frustration to God, we can leave it with God.

The psalmist concludes in verses 23-24 by inviting God to search him through and through. It is as if, by writing the psalm, the psalmist has convinced himself that this is the safe and right thing to do!

How safe do you feel about asking God to do the same?

We can easily tell ourselves that God is holding back from us, when actually it is us who are holding back from God. An awareness of how imperfect we are can make us fear to have God too close (verse 1). The psalmist knows that God sees all his actions (verse 3), hears all his words (verse 4), and even knows the inner thoughts of his heart (verse 2)! But he also knows that God is his creator, and that the meaning of his life is found in God (verse 16). Therefore he invites God's scrutiny (verses 23-24) for he knows that a full life is a life spent in an honest relationship with God.

Your Notes

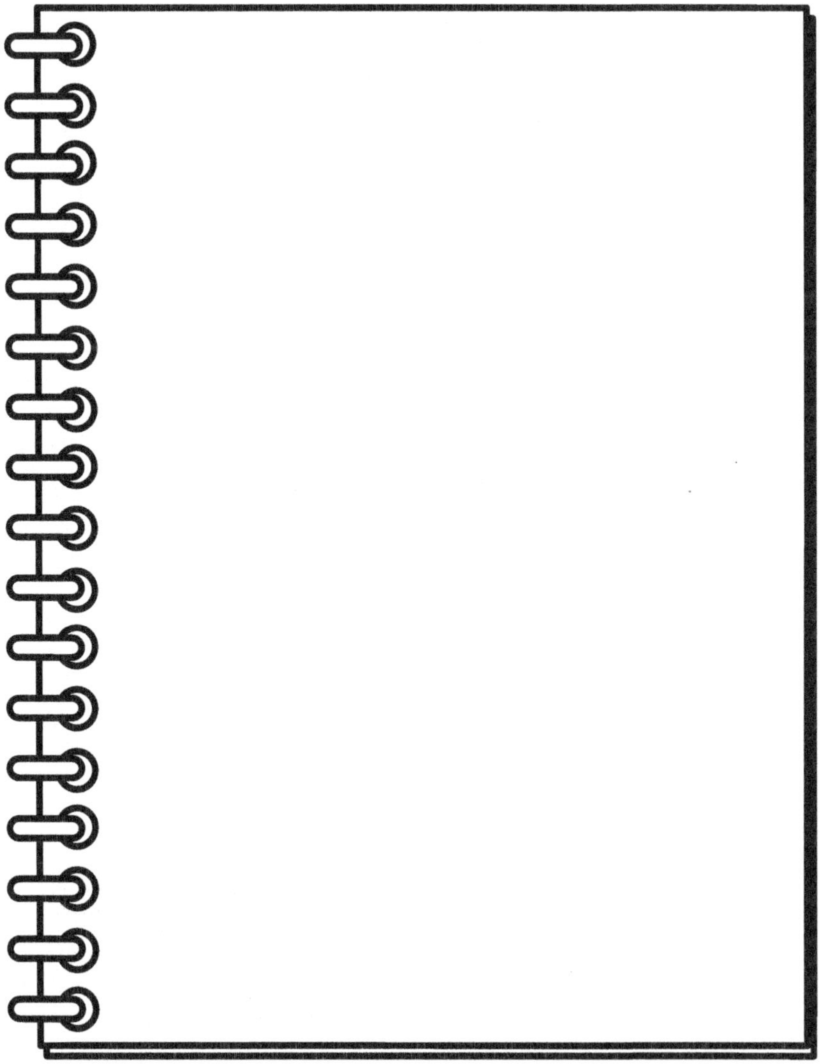

Reflection

But...
I Don't Feel Like I Have a Personal Relationship With God

What does a personal relationship with God feel like –
being known in a complete and absolute way?
I know I can hide nothing and nowhere –
but the fear of letting God in close looms heavy.

Being known in a complete and absolute way –
opening my heart to expose raw honesty within.
The fear of letting God in close looms heavy –
but whatever I feel, I can trust in Him!

Opening my heart to expose raw honesty within –
I know I can hide nothing and nowhere!
Whatever I feel, I can trust in Him –
that's what a personal relationship with God feels like!

M. McKinnell

In Deep

Ideas for Responding in Prayer

Ready to dabble:

Quick and simple prayer ideas

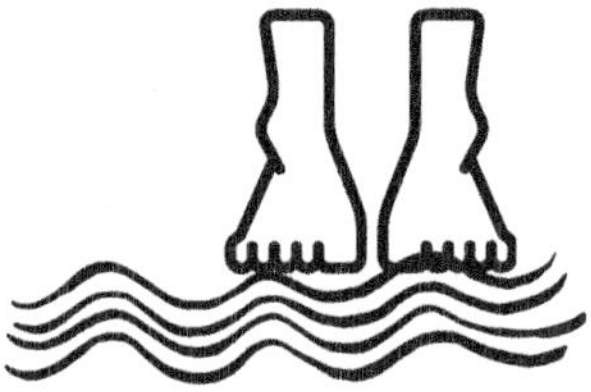

Verse 5 of the Psalm speaks about God laying His hand on the psalmist. In a quiet place, place one hand on the top of your head and close your eyes. Take some time to notice how that feels. Now imagine God scanning your body from top to toe, just like that airport security scanner. Imagine any negative or sinful thoughts and feelings are flowing up through your head and into the hand you have placed on top. Then 'give' them to God. God can handle them.

Going deeper:

Ideas to try if you have more time

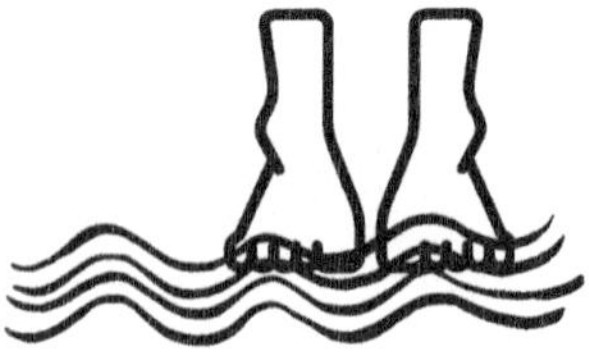

Using some 'scratch art' paper (this can be purchased cheaply from most craft shops, or you can make your own using wax crayons and poster paint) sractch the words of Psalm 139:12 into your paper, prayerfully reflecting on the verse as you do so.
You make want to make this into a piece of art that you can put somewhere visible, to remind you of God's closeness every day.

Space for Journalling

Diving right in:

Ideas for personal prayer and journalling

Create your own version of this Psalm, or rewrite it in your own words. If you need some guidance, work your way through the following sentence starters:

God, you are so powerful, like.....

You are with me in the morning, when I....

You are with me through the day when I...

You are with me in the evening when I...

The whole world is full of your presence. You can be found... and...

You were there when I visited... and...

You knew me before I was born, and you can see my future when I hope to be....

Your thoughts are higher than mine. If I could ask you one question it would be....

When people are unkind about my faith in you, I feel...

God, I want to get to know you because...

Space for Journalling

Games and Ideas for Groups

Portraits

Sit the young people in a circle and give each one a piece of paper and a selection of drawing materials. Challenge them to draw a portrait of someone else in the circle, without revealing whom they have chosen - but only given them 30 seconds to do it! After 30 seconds it's pencils-down, and the young people must guess who each portrait is supposed to be.

For an even funnier version of this game, give the young people a piece of card painted with wet PVA glue and selection of dried pasta shapes and spaghetti with which to make their portraits. (They may need longer than 30 seconds to make their 'creations' if you do this version!)

This game can lead into a discussion on how we see ourselves versus how God/other people see us.

Prayer Labyrinth

A prayer labyrinth or a finger-prayer-labyrinth works well with Psalm 139, as the Psalm has a chiastic structure - that is, one that leads in and then out again. Various finger labyrinths are available for free online, or the young people may wish to draw one of their own design. Full size prayer-labyrinths can be rented, or created using masking tape, lines of pebbles, or drawn/painted onto large dust-sheets or ground-sheets laid on the floor.

Read the Psalm slowly, up to verse 13, on the way into the centre of the labyrinth, pause there, reflecting on verse 14, then read verses 15 to the end on the way out.

Ideas for All Age Worship

If the young people have done the exercise from 'Diving Right In' (i.e. writing their own version of the Psalm) then this can be shared in various ways during collective worship. It may be better to have the whole congregation read the Psalm responsively, rather than having one or more young people read it from the front, to prevent it becoming a performance rather than an act of worship.

Likewise, finger-labyrinths are really easy and effective to use for All Age worship. (NB: Full size prayer labyrinths can present some logistical difficulties for a large congregation, and very young worshippers may find it difficult to use them in a slow, reflective kind of way!)

Mirror tiles can be purchased cheaply in large packs from DIY stores. During the teaching time, ask the congregation to point out and name any symbols/markers of God's presence in the room, i.e. cross, banners, Bibles. Then ask them to look in the mirrors, and remember that each of us is a symbol of God's presence in the world too.
Many people find it uncomfortable to look at their own reflection when not in private. Acknowledge that discomfort - and use it to lead into a time of prayer focussed on self-examination and repentance.
You may wish to provide each member of the congregation with a permanant marker. Ask them to write the words "I am fearfully and wonderfully made" on their mirror tile, and take it home for personal prayer and reflection.

Bible Study 2

But...

...what if God is angry at me?

Who likes a good sing-song?

Zephaniah 3:14-20

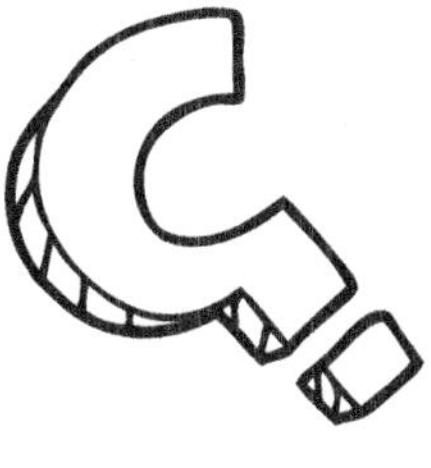

Look again at Zephaniah 3:17 for the answer.

Who do you go to for help when you feel you've messed up?

In the time of the prophet Zephaniah, God's people (also called 'Daughter Zion*' in this Bible passage) knew they had messed up, and the consequences were pressing hard upon them.

For decades, under the rule of King Manasseh, they had forgotten the ways of God and tried to copy the worship, dishonest trading and agressive foreign policies of their neighbours. Far from buying them a seat at the cool kid's table, this had left the nation broken and in conflict, highly vulnerable to invasion, cowering in the shadow of the massive (and rapidly-expanding) Assyrian Empire.

God's people were afraid. They had let God down, and now their enemies were closing in. Could they go to God for help?

Can you think of a time when you messed up, and needed to go to an adult for help?

How did it feel, admitting that you had made a mistake?

What kind of a reaction did you expect?

Did the person you went to react in the way you thought they would?

In Zephaniah's time, the people only turned back to God because they were afraid of their enemies. How do you think God should have dealt with them?

*'Zion' is.a symbolic name, which sometimes refers to the city of Jerusalem, and sometimes has a deeper, spiritual meaning - referring to the people of God or the Hevenly City in the New Creation.

Your Notes

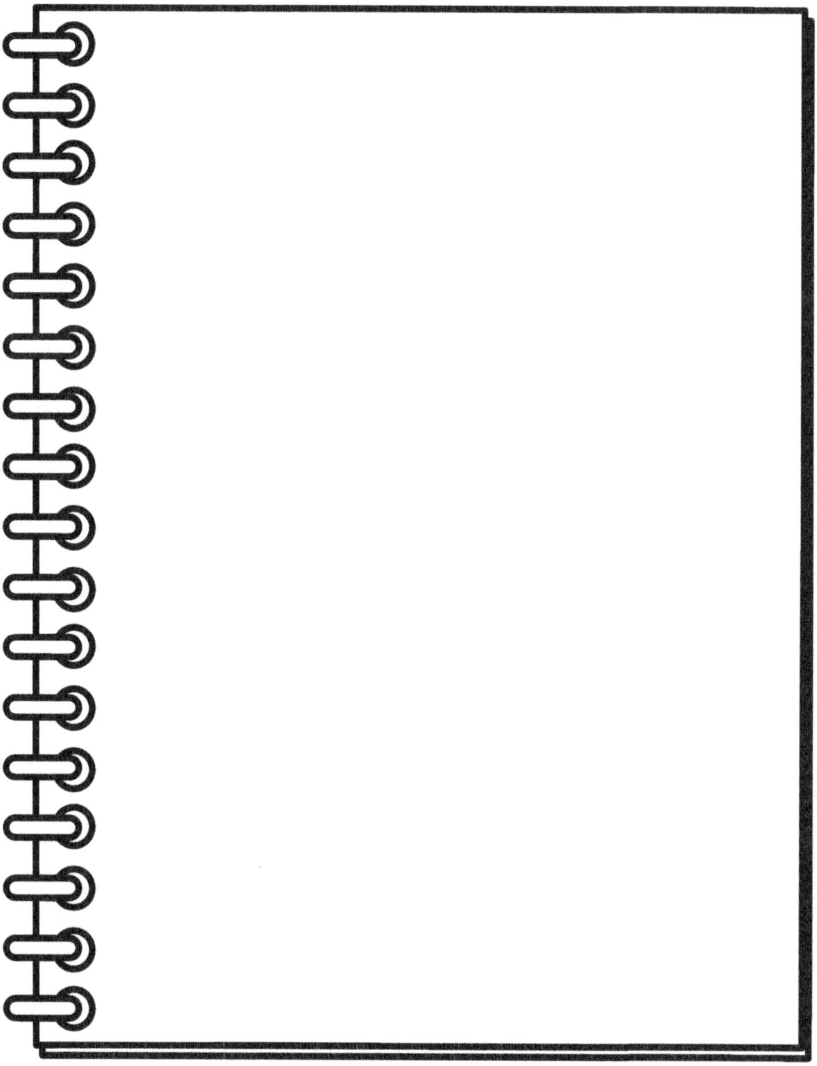

Look at verse 15. Where do the people find God? What names is God given in this verse?

What two things is God described as doing in verse 15?

If you were God, do you think you would have done the same?

Turn to Matthew 20:1-16

In Matthew 20:9, how much did the 'eleventh hour' workers get paid? What about those who were employed at the first hour (verse 10)?

What would you have paid the workers if you were the vineyard's owner?

It's starting to look like God just doesn't do *fair,* right? Well, in some ways that's true - mercy and fairness are not the same thing.

Turn to Psalm 103:10-11 - what reason does the psalmist give for God's mercy?

Turn back to Zephaniah 3:17. Here, God is described again as being amongst the people. The image is one of a mother singing a lullaby to a child.

In Hebrew, the Old Testament usually refers to God using male pronouns (he/him). But of course, God is God, and does not have to be thought of as one particular gender or sex! Genesis 1:27 refers to both men and women being created in God's image, and female metaphors for God can be found in both the Old and New Testaments. (See: Hosea 11:3-4; Hosea 13:8; Deuteronomy 32; Isaiah 66:13; Matthew 23:37; Luke 15:8-10.) How does it feel for you to think of God as a mother figure rather than a father figure?

Your Notes

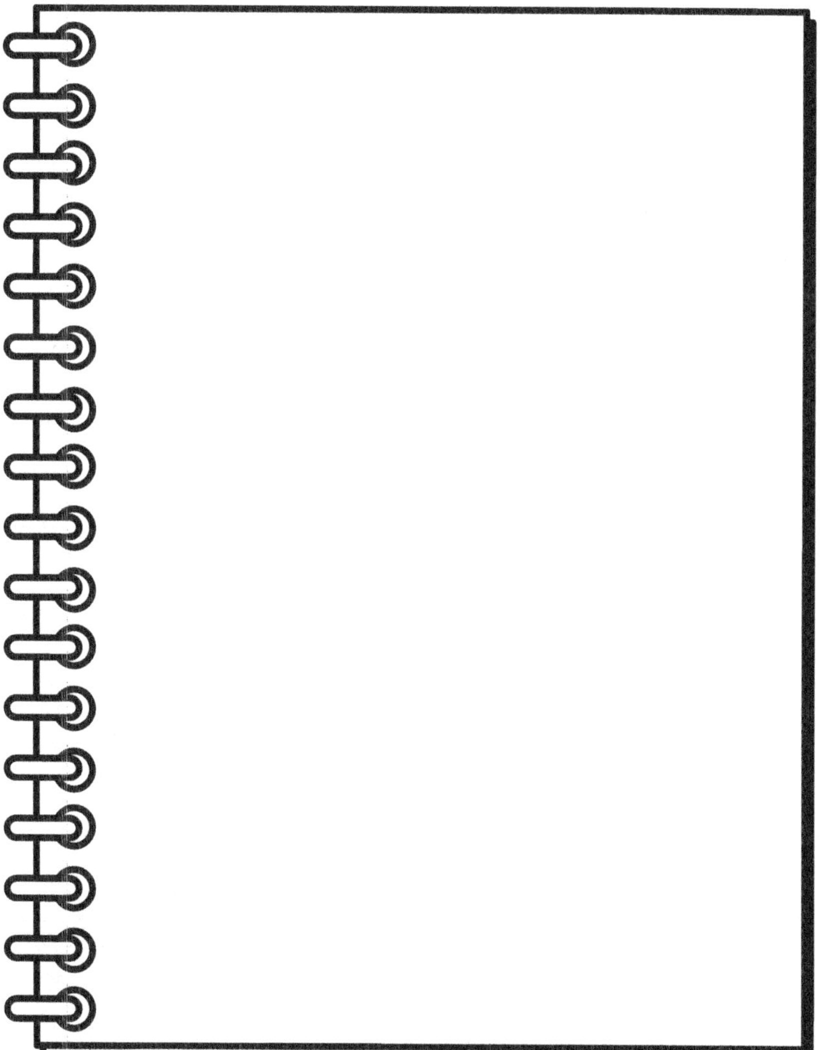

Can you think of a time when you felt peer pressured into doing something you knew was wrong? Maybe you didn't want to join in with cruel gossip at school or in your workplace? Maybe you stood up for someone being bullied and were bullied yourself as a result? Or maybe you were too afraid to speak out and went along with what the group was doing, feeling guilty all the time?

The meaning of verse 18 is uncertain, because the Hebrew is difficult to translate. My own translation is this:

"I will gather those of you who have been saddened by the way the people have worshipped. [I will gather] the ones who have been scorned."

Compare the translation of this verse in some different types of Bible. Which translation do you like best and why? Is God angry at the people who have been quietly wishing that everyone would turn back God?

How much do you think worrying about what other people will think, or about how other people will treat you, affects the way you approach your faith and God?

In verses 18-20 God promises to do a number of things for the people now that they have turned back. Make a list of God's promises. If you were God, do you think you would do the same?

As humans we are not always very merciful towards each other. We tend to judge others harshly, and it is easy to project that onto God and feel like God must be judging us harshly too. But the Bible paints a very different picture of God, one that is more like a forgiving parent than a judging friend. Getting that picture right in our own minds can help us to feel safe and confident about having a personal relationship with our creator.

Your Notes

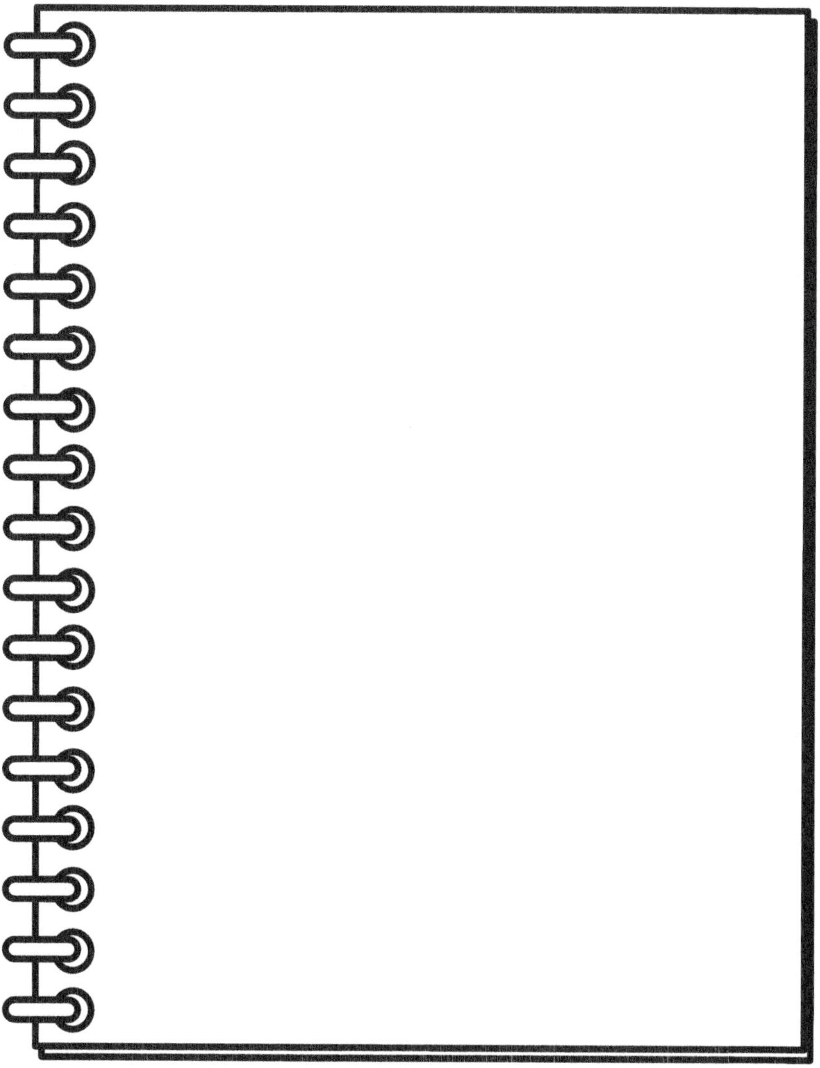

Reflection

But...
I Don't Feel Like I Have a Personal Relationship With God

When Jerusalem forgot the ways of God
she was broken, in conflict and highly vulnerable;
the city, all her people, had let God down –
not one went willingly against the trend.

She was broken, in conflict and highly vulnerable –
now her enemies were closing in;
not one went willingly against the trend –
afraid, she draws back to God as last resort.

Now her enemies were closing in –
expecting God judging, she finds God forgiving;
afraid, she draws back to God at last resort –
God's safety, peace and confidence so very unexpected.

Expecting God judging, she finds God forgiving –
The city, all her people, had let God down;
God's safety, peace and confidence so very unexpected,
when Jerusalem forgot the ways of God.

M. McKinnell

In Deep

Ideas for Responding in Prayer

Ready to dabble:

Quick and simple prayer ideas

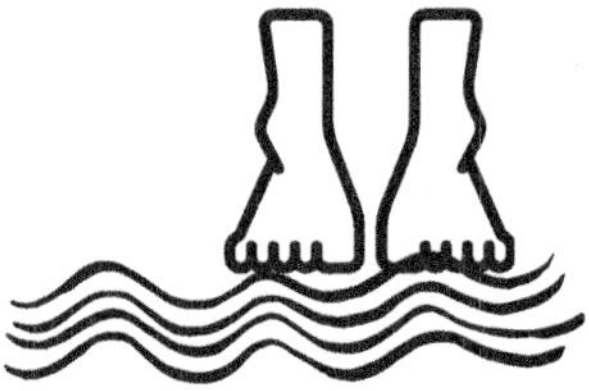

Take a blob of plasticine or blue-tack and form it, slowly, into the shape of a cross, whilst reflecting on the words of Psalm 51:1-6.

Then, moving on to Psalm 51:7-12, re-form the plasticine cross into the shape of a heart.

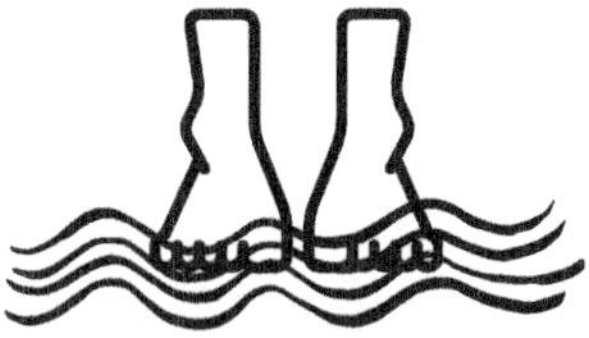

Going deeper:

Ideas to try if you have more time

The assumption of God as male can have more of an affect on our relationship than we realise. For some people this creates an unnecessary barrier against growing close to God.

Try writing out one or more of the following passages using she/her or they/them pronouns instead of the traditional use of he/him. How does it feel to see and hear God spoken of with different pronouns?

- Psalm 23:1-3
- Exodus 15:1-3
- Psalm 50:1-6
- Psalm 103:8-13

Space for Journalling

Diving right in:

Ideas for personal prayer and journalling

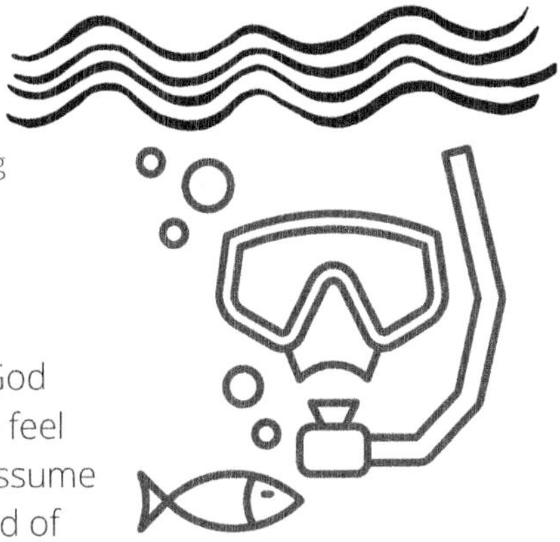

- Read Matthew 7:1-5

Sometimes we hold back from God because we know how angry we feel towards other people, and we assume that God must feel the same kind of anger towards us.

It may be helpful to take some time to address any anger or resentment towards others that we might be feeling.

- Draw a number of 'specks' in your prayer journal, and amongst them make a note of things and people that are currently irritating or angering you.

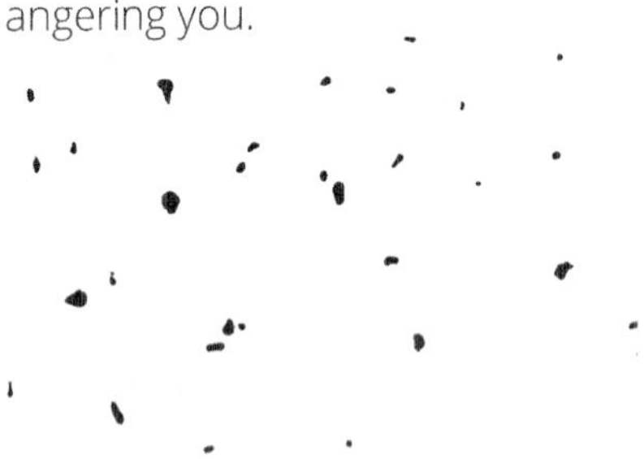

- Now draw a large plank, and in it write down anything you think God might be angry about towards you.

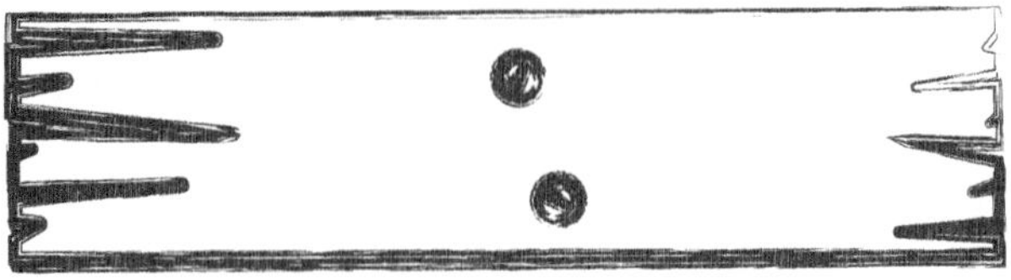

- Turn to 1 John 1:5-10 and reflect on these verses, offering up your own sin to God's mercy.

Space for Journalling

Games and Ideas for Groups

Balloon Pop

Divide the young people into two (or more) teams and give each team a set of inflated balloons of one particular colour. When the game starts, each team must keep their own balloons up in the air while at the same time trying to ground and pop any of the other team(s)' balloons. No one is allowed to catch or hold any balloons to stop them falling to the ground. The winning team is the last team to have any balloons un-popped, or the team with the most surviving balloons at the end of an allotted time period. Lead this into a discussion about how difficult it is to keep an eye on your own balloons while chasing down the other teams' balloons! It is the same with sin - it is difficult to hear God speaking into our own lives if we are too busy judging other people on God's behalf. (See Matthew 7:1-5)

The Moral High Ground

Stand one young person on a step-stool or chair (not too high!) and a second person on the ground facing them. Give them each end of a broom handle (or similar) to hold. By pulling/pushing the broom handle, the person on the ground must try to pull the other person off the chair or the person on the chair must try to push the person on the ground off their feet. The person on the chair/step will almost always lose. Lead this into a discussion on how "pride comes before a fall" (Proverbs 16:18), perhaps also reflecting on 1 Corinthians 10:12-13.

God of Surprises

Stand the young people in a circle with one person in the middle. They must throw a soft ball to someone in the circle, saying "catch" or "drop" as they throw. Whoever is receiving the ball must do the opposite of what the thrower says, i.e. they must catch it if the thrower calls "drop".
Lead this into a discussion about how God's mercy can feel unexpected, or counter-intuitive at times. You could look at the story of Zaccheaus (Luke 19:1-10) or the Woman at the Well (John 4:1-26) as an example.

Ideas for All Age Worship

The 'Moral High Ground' activity from the Games and Ideas for Groups section can be used as a demonstration in front of the congregation, leading into a talk on Matthew 7:1-5 or on Proverbs 16:18.

The idea of 'planks versus specks' can also be adapted. Members of the congregation could be asked to add their fingerprint to a large sheet of paper on the way in to the service. (Ink pads can be purchased cheaply online, or from most craft shops). During the service, the completed sheet of fingerprints can be held up, and each fingerprint said to represent a 'speck' - that is, some small way in which each person has annoyed/angered someone else. However, Jesus taught us to let God take care of these 'specks' and instead pay attention to our 'planks'. At this point, two volunteers could be asked to bring in two large planks of wood and put them together to form the shape of the cross, leading into some prayers of confession and reconciliation.

A different approach to this topic is to focus on God's grace and mercy. Either as they arrive, or at a certain point in the service, start giving out small gifts to everyone in the congregation. The young people might like to make and distribute these gifts themselves - perhaps small posies of flowers or parcels of chocolates.
Ask the members of the congregation to think what they have done that might have prompted the young people to give them gifts. See if you can get a few people to volunteer ideas. Once everyone has had time to puzzle over the gifts, tell them that they actually haven't done anything to earn them at all! These gifts are a symbol of God's grace, freely given.

Bible Study 3

But...
...Nothing 'happens' when I Pray!

Can you pray for it not rain on your wedding day?

James 5:7-18

Look again at James 5:17 for the answer.

The epistle of James was one of the first parts of the New Testament to be written. It was written for a group of people who had been following the Jewish religion - so they were used to living by a lot of rules! However, now that they had become followers of Jesus their lives were to be governed by grace instead of rules. But would God still answer their prayers if they weren't keeping to lots of rules? How could they gain God's favour with their new way of life?

When you pray, what do you wish would happen?

How does this compare with what actually happens?

When Jesus ascended into heaven, Luke records that some angels promised Jesus would one day return. You can read about what the angels said in Acts chapter 1. Many believers thought this would happen really soon, but we are still waiting for the event today! In James 5:7-9, James writes a note for the believers who are impatient for Jesus to return.

What does James tell the believers to *be?*

What does James tell the believers to *do?*

And what does James caution the believers against in verse 9?

Waiting for things is not always easy - whether you're waiting for a birthday or the last day of school or for meeting the love of your life! It's especially hard when you don't know how long you might be waiting for.

What difference does it make when you *finally* get something after a very long wait?

Your Notes

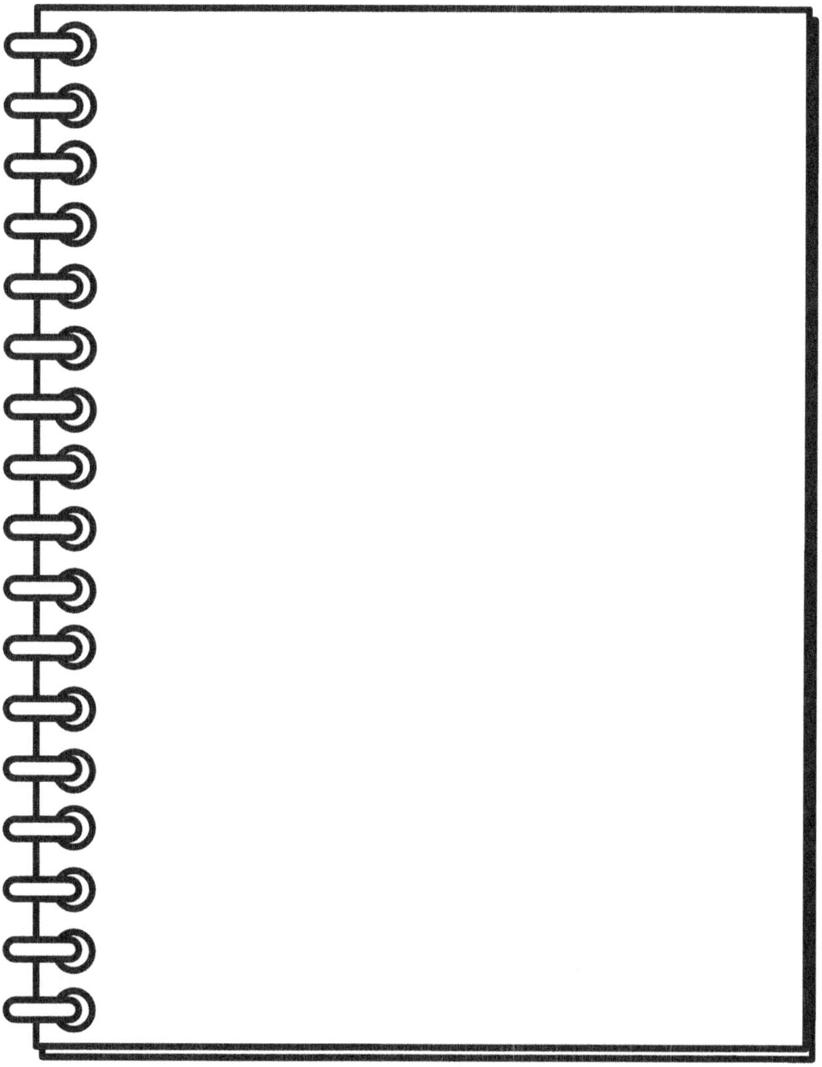

Look up the word 'patient' in a dictionary. You can see there that sometimes it is an adjective but sometimes it is also a noun. As a noun, it is linked with suffering and being helpless.

In Acts 16:22-25 two of Jesus' followers, Paul and Silas, found themselves helpless in prison. How did they respond to their situation? (Acts 16:25) Read on a little further in Acts 16 to find out how God responded to their faithfulness.

Paul and Silas set us a great example, but who else does James suggest as a role model for us? (Look at James 5:10)

Are there other people in your own life right now who set you a good example? Do you think God could have put those people around you?

In verse 11 James mentions **Job**. You can find his story in the old Testament book named after him. It is important to know that Job was almost certainly **not** a real person; his story is a fable that was told to help God's people learn to be faithful.

Read chapter 1 of Job, noting verse 22 in particular. Do you think your attitude and actions would have been the same as Job's?

In Job 27:1-6 we hear him speak for himself. What does Job resolve to do, or actually *not do*, in the midst of his suffering? Make a list of the things he mentions in Job 27:1-6.

Your Notes

When Job was suffering, all his friends abandoned him or blamed him. Have you ever had a 'fair weather friend' - someone who was only being friendly to you because there was something in it for them? Maybe you had food to share, or they needed a lift to a party?

In Job 27:1-6 we learn than a true friend of God is someone who stays faithful even when things don't seem to be going their way.

How does James describe God in James 5:11? Does God sound like someone to whom it is worth being a true friend?

In verse 11 James also mentions God's purposes. Do you think God's purposes are always the same as our own?

It is easy to fall into the trap of making 'deals' with God. Like, "I'll believe in you if you answer this prayer..." but in verse 12 James cautions us about that kind of thinking. Look at Luke 9:57-62 to see what Jesus said about making a decision to follow him.

James encouraged the believers to be decisive about following Jesus, but he also knew that wouldn't be easy. The Christian life is full of highs and lows. What kinds of highs and lows does James list in verses 13-16?

What does James advise the believers to do in each situation? Why do you think it is a good idea to pray with other believers sometimes rather than always on your own?

What was the last thing you prayed about? Or, if you had to pray right now, what would you pray about?

Can you match up your prayer with anything James lists in verses 13-16?

Your Notes

Verse 16 is a little tricky to translate. It could mean, "The prayer of a righteous person is powerful and effective." But it could also mean, "The effective prayer of a righteous person is powerful as it is working."

Try looking up the verse in a few different translations.

Which do you think is the best translation and why?

In verses 17-18, James alludes to the story of a respected prophet, Elijah. You can read this section of Elijah's story in the book of 1 Kings, chapters 17 and 18.

What does James say about Elijah at the start of verse 17?

Does this affect your choice of translation for James 5:16?

In Luke 11:1-4 Jesus teaches the disciples how to pray, but what story does Jesus tell immediately after teaching the Lord's Prayer? (Luke 11:5-8)

How easy do you find it to persist when answers to prayer are a long time coming?

Prayer is a great way to develop our relationship with God. (Some might say it is the only way!) Prayer encourages us to be persistent, because not all prayers are answered quickly. Prayer also helps us to keep in relationship with other believers, if we are brave enough to be open and honest with them about what we are praying for! It is good to pray with friends, and also to have role models. Who do you know that prays in a powerful and effective way?

Your Notes

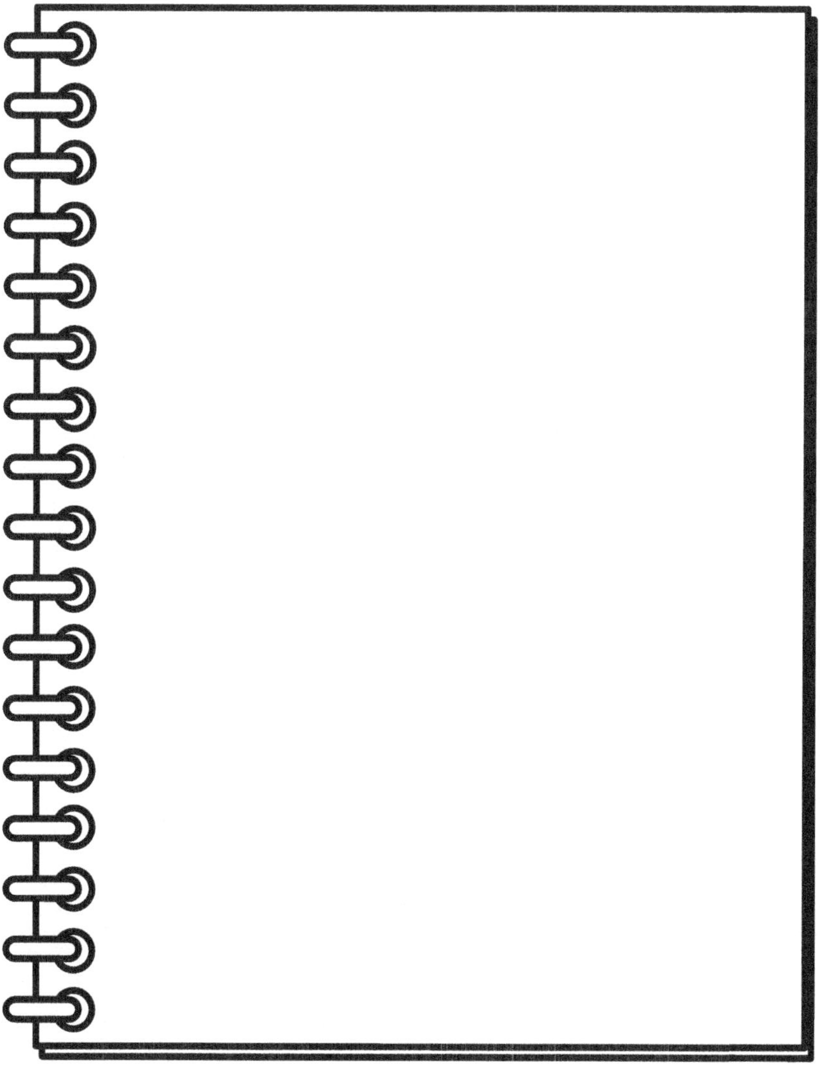

Reflection

But...
I Don't Feel Like I Have a Personal Relationship With God

We persist in our prayers – in the good times and bad –
yet the nagging doubts grow when it feels nothing 'happens'.
Waiting for God's remains our biggest challenge –
the temptation to strike a deal grows stronger each minute!

The nagging doubts grow when it feels nothing 'happens' –
our wait might be seconds, days or eternity.
The temptation to strike a deal grows stronger each minute –
our persistence required as we patiently wait!

Our wait might be seconds, days or eternity –
still, we stay brave and open and honest.
Our persistence required as we patiently wait –
God will reward our patience and faithfulness.

Still, we stay brave and open and honest –
waiting for God's remains our biggest challenge.
God will reward our patience and faithfulness –
we persist in our prayers – in the good times and bad!

M. McKinnell

In Deep

Ideas for Responding in Prayer

Ready to dabble:

Quick and simple prayer ideas

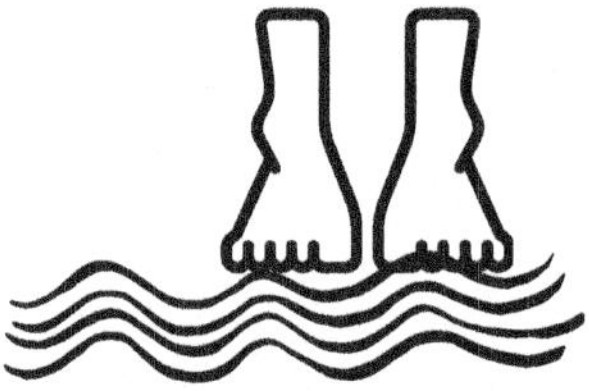

Look at a copy of the Lord's Prayer in whatever version is familiar from your Church community. Read it slowly and underline any words or phrases that jump out at you.

It could be things you don't feel you understand, things you haven't noticed or considered before, or things that feel particularly meaningful to you at that moment.

If appropriate, spend some time sharing in a group what you have underlined and why. Or, start a prayer journal where you record your experiences.

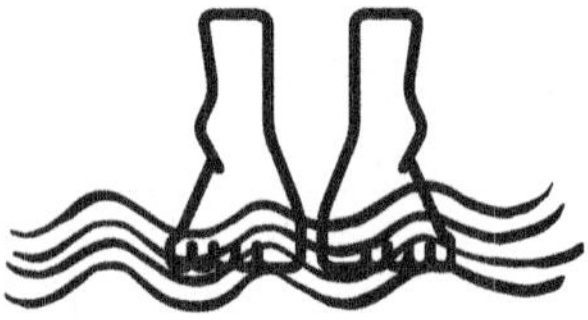

Going deeper:

Ideas to try if you have more time

Many Christian groups and communities pray the Lord's Prayer daily. If this is not already a part of your prayer life then why not try it for a week or two? Get some friends to join you! Agree a time of day when everyone will pause what they are doing for a minute to say the prayer. You could set phone reminders, or nominate someone to send out reminders by text. You may like to make notes in your prayer journal about how you feel before and after stopping to pray each day. Does pausing each day to say the Lord's Prayer make a difference?

Space for Journalling

Diving right in:

Ideas for personal prayer and journalling

Christians can easily slip into the habit of *thinking* a lot about praying without ever actually doing it! Few of us are able to set aside hours and hours for quiet contemplation, so the best way to start, and sustain, a prayer life is to pick some small, regular habits which are easy to keep to.

Having a small 'prayer station' at home can help. You could set up a little corner with a world map, some post-it notes, a candle, a Bible and some paper for journalling. Then, pick a time of day (perhaps first thing in the morning or last thing at night) where you can (safely) light the candle and spend a few minutes just focussing on God. It doesn't have to be long - a little every day is easy to stick to and remember.

(And don't lose heart if you miss a day: one should never let the perfect spoil the good!)

If you prefer more structured prayer, then there are numerous books, email lists and apps for daily prayer. Try a few out to see what you like, and don't forget to keep a journal of how things are going so that one day you can look back and see how far you've come!

Space for Journalling

Games and Ideas for groups

Prayer Stations

Time spent with interactive prayer activities can be helpful for young people who don't connect with long, wordy prayers or long stretches of silence. There are many ideas for interactive prayer stations all over the internet! The ideas out there are of varying quality, and some will work better with one group than with another, so it may be good to get the young people themselves to do the research and choose some activities that they think will be meaningful to them.

The Patience Game

This is a simple game about waiting. Make sure there are no audible clocks in the room, and that anyone wearing a watch has it covered up. Everyone must close their eyes, except for one timekeeper, and put their hand in the air (as silently as possible, so that others don't hear the movement) whenever they think 3 minutes has elapsed. Some people will be quite accurate and some will be wildly off! Talk about how it feels to be waiting, trying to mark time. Are there some situations, (like when you are watching a favourite TV programme,) when three minutes goes by really quickly? Are there other times, (perhaps when you are standing at a bus stop in the cold!) when three minutes goes very slowly? What kind of strategies do the young people employ to help pass the time?

The Blind Prayer Experiment

The week before your youth group meets, say a simple prayer every day for each of the young people in your group, asking God to bless them and protect them. Do this without telling the young people about it before the meeting. Then, when you meet, tell them that you have prayed for each of them all week, and ask the young people if they can think of one thing that has happened that week that could have been an answer to your prayer. This will probably spark some interesting conversations about what kind of things God does/does not do in our lives!

Ideas for All Age Worship

The Lord's Prayer activity from the 'In Deep' section can work well in all age Worship, encouraging people to slow down and focus on the meaning of the Lord's Prayer, instead of just rattling it off from memory. If you have the space, and a willing congregation (!), you could display each line of the Lord's Prayer on posters around the room, and ask people to move towards the poster with the line that they feel most drawn to that day.

Interactive prayer stations or activities are also a great way to engage all generations with praying. Perhaps the young people could take responsibility for choosing and setting up some activities for the rest of the congregation? Many interactive prayer ideas can be done without the need for people to leave their seats, if your facilities don't allow for this.

The young people could undertake the 'Blind Prayer Experiment' on behalf of the Church, committing to pray every day for the members of your congregation in the week leading up to All Age Worship. Then, at the service, encourage everyone to share things that they think may have been answers to the young peoples' prayers for them.

Bible Study 4

But...
...I'll never keep it up!

What is the best prize
you could ever win?

Philippians 3:8-21

Look again at Philippians
3:14 for the answer.

Paul is in prison! We have already seen, in the previous study, how Paul passed the time when he was behind bars. (Turn to Acts 16:25 if you need a quick reminder.) Here, Paul writes to the Philippians to say that he is overflowing with joy, because he knows they are persevering with living Christ's way, even though he cannot be there to encourage and guide them.

But persevering in the Christian life is hard, even with a great role model like Paul to inspire us. Philippians is a letter full of encouragement and advice on how to live a life of faith. The whole letter is worth reading (it is quite short!) but in this study we will look specifically at Philippians 3:8-21.

If you could see into your own future, what do you think you would see? Make a list of the top 3 things you want to achieve in your life.

Now look at what Paul says in Philippians 3:8. How does Paul's list look next to yours?

If following Christ was not at the top of your list, what do you think would have to happen to put it there?

Look at verses 9-11. What things does Paul think he gains from being in relationship with Christ?

Paul says in verse 10 that he even wants to suffer and die like Jesus did! Look at Philippians 1:12-13. You can see there that Paul is glad to be in prison, because he can spread the gospel to the guards.

Paul may be referring to the fact that, when Jesus died on the cross, the Roman guards nearby said, "Surely he was the son of God!" (Matthew 27:54).

Your Notes

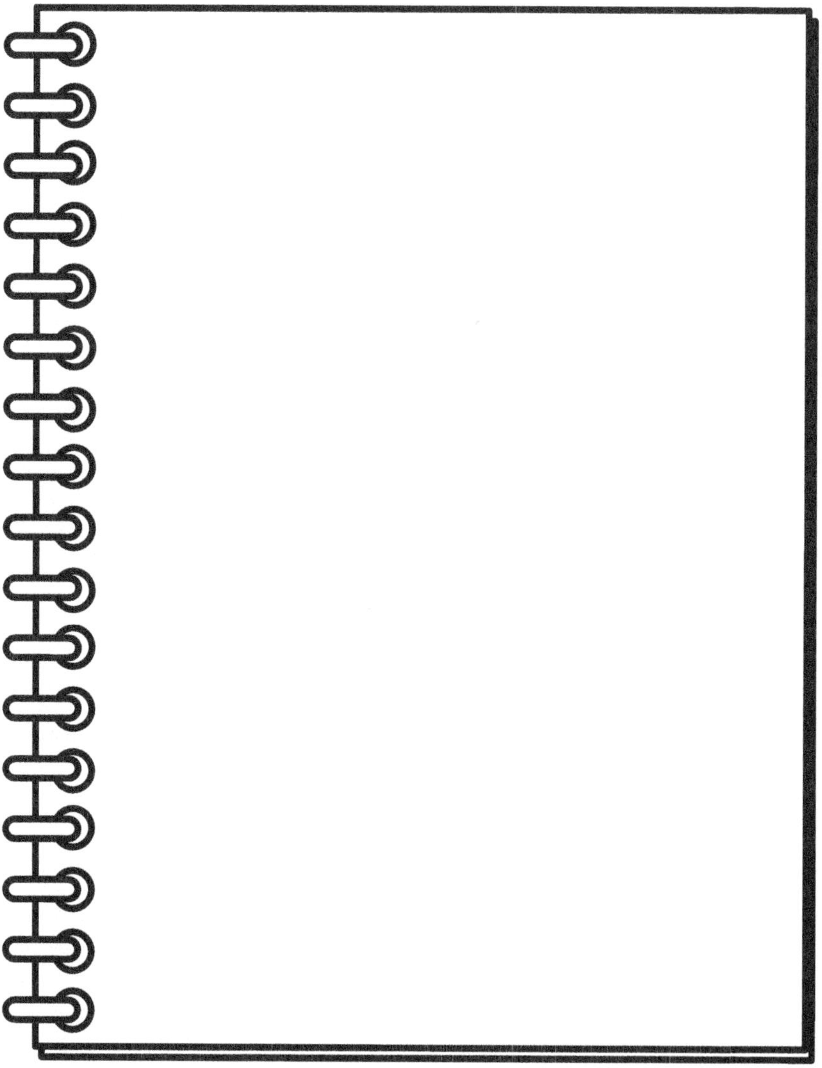

Do you think you could ever welcome hardship the way Paul did, if you knew it was spreading the Good News about Jesus?

In some parts of the world, Christians are still persecuted and killed for their faith. But even in countries where that is not likely to happen, people can still suffer bullying, discrimination and harassment because of their faith. Do you sometimes see this kind of thing happening in your own context?

What does Paul expect to gain from living the life of faith? (Verse 11)

In verse 12 Paul admits that, like any of us, he isn't perfect. But what reason does he give in verse 12 for persevering anyway? Look at John 15:16 for Jesus' own way of saying this.

Keeping going is tough, but in verses 13 and 14 Paul tells us how he sustains his forward progress. What three things does he do?

*Flower = emergency colouring in.

In verse 14 Paul refers again to the 'prize' or goal of all his faithfulness. Does this prize excite you?

What are some other good things about living the Christian life? Check out these Bible passages for some ideas:

- Philippians 4:6-7
- Isaiah 40:29-31
- John 14:27
- Psalm 23
- Psalm 68:5-6

Your Notes

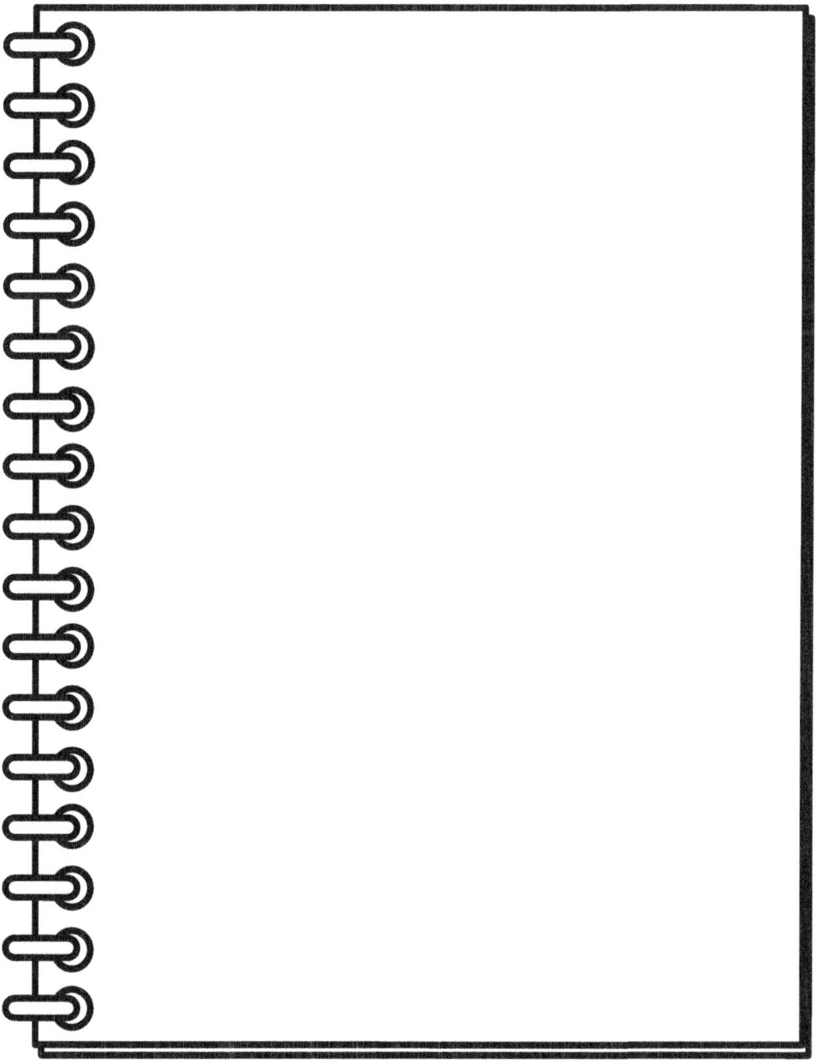

In verse 15 Paul suggests that living a life of faith is a sign of 'maturity', do you agree? By contrast, what does Paul think is 'immature' or not worth striving for? (Verse 19)

As young people (and even as not-so-young people!) it is easy to obsess about our bodies, always thinking about how we look and about the appetites that drive us. But how does Paul describe the body in verse 21?

Turn to Matthew 6:25-34.

In verse 25, what does Jesus tell us not to worry about?

What reasons does Jesus give in verses 26-30?

What does Jesus tell us to focus on instead? (Verse 33) Does this sound siimilar to what Paul has been saying to the Philippians?

Jesus tells us not to worry about tomorrow, and Paul has told us to forget what lies behind. So, what does that leave us with?

What does Paul tell us to do in the present moment in Philippians 4:1?

In the opening chapter of Philippians (chapter 1, verse 6) Paul expresses confidence that once God has started to work in someone's life, God will not leave the job half done.

Even if we get distracted, take a wrong turn, or lose our momentum for a little while, the 'upward call of Christ' stays on our lives. The very fact that you have engaged with these studies suggests that the call is there - even if you have faith 'as small as a mustard seed' (Matthew 17:20-21). So do not worry about whether you will keep it up tomorrow, but why not take a moment to make today count!

Your Notes

Reflection

But...
I Don't Feel Like I Have a Personal Relationship With God

Can we really see this faith journey through
with all our distractions, fears, and wrong turns?
The fear that we will give up remains always present,
yet God does not leave the job half done.

Despite all our distractions, fears, and wrong turns,
encouragement and advice lovingly comes our way.
God does not leave the job half done –
the difference we make spreads God's joy around.

Encouragement and advice lovingly comes our way –
the upward call of Christ stays in our lives.
The difference we make spreads God's joy around
as we take a moment to make today count.

The upward call of Christ stays in our lives.
The fear that we will give up remains always present,
yet as we take a moment to make today count –
yes, we will see this faith journey through!

M. McKinnell

In Deep

Ideas for Responding in Prayer

Ready to dabble:

Quick and simple prayer ideas

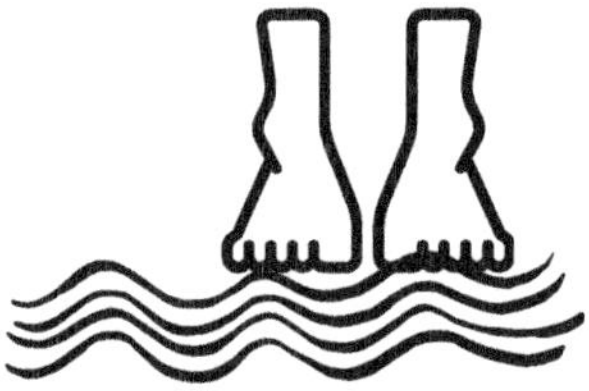

In the Methodist Church there is a special service once per year where worshippers use this prayer to re-dedicate their lives to God. Try saying the prayer and making your own act of rededication.

I am no longer my own but yours.
Put me to what you will,
rank me with whom you will;
put me to doing,
put me to suffering;
let me be employed for you,
or laid aside for you,
exalted for you,
or brought low for you;
let me be full,
let me be empty,
let me have all things,
let me have nothing:
I freely and wholeheartedly yield all things
to your pleasure and disposal.
And now, glorious and blessed God,
Father, Son and Holy Spirit,
you are mine and I am yours.
So be it.
And the covenant now made on earth,
let it be ratified in heaven.

(The Methodist Covenant Prayer)

Space for Journalling

Going deeper:

Ideas to try if you have more time

Psalm 23 tells the story of following God from the perspective of ...a sheep!
You are (probably) not a sheep, so what does the same Psalm look like from your perspective? What is your equivalent of green pastures? (Think of a place where you are fed and nurtured.) Or still waters? (Think of a place where you are safe and refreshed.)

Either individually, or in a group, try writing your own version of the Psalm. What does discipleship look like in your context?

Diving right in:

Ideas for personal prayer and journalling

Even though he knows he is not perfect, Paul knows he is a role model for the Philippians.

What role models do you have in your Christian life?

Do they *know* they are your role models?

Do you think *you* might be a role model for someone? Perhaps a younger sibling or friends around you are looking at your life as an example for their own. What do you think about the example you set? Spend some time reflecting on this in your journal, asking God to help you in the example you set to others.

If possible, make some time to meet with your role models. Ask them about how they sustain their life of faith, what their patterns of personal prayer are, and about how. they follow the way of Jesus in their daily lives.

Space for Journalling

Games and Ideas for groups

The Prize

Choose a really good prize for this game - something like a large bar of chocolate that most young people would be keen to win! Show the prize, then ask the young people to stand with their arms stretched above their heads. When you say "go" they must lower their arms slowly to make a T-shape, like Jesus on the cross. The young people must then hold that position as long as possible, without anything supporting their arms. After a while their shoulders will start to hurt! Allow the young people to give up one-by-one, until the last person to keep their T is the winner - and they get the prize. Lead into a discussion on persevering, and waiting, even when it is *literally* painful!

Yesterday, Today and Tomorrow

Sort the young people into a circle, divided into groups of 6-8 if you have a large number. Going around the circle, each person must list an answer to prayer, or just a happy experience, that happened to them yesterday, one that happened today, and one that they hope for tomorrow. It could be really simple things like not getting homework or spending time with their pet. Once everyone has shared, someone should be picked at random, and their task is to recall what everyone else's three things were! Let them keep going until they make a mistake, then ask someone else to try. Can anyone remember them all? Lead into a discussion on how we should not worry about yesterday or tomorrow, but instead focus on our lives today.

Working Together

In a very large (not breakable) bowl, make a big, beautiful ice cream sundae. Then ask for two volunteers to eat it! However, there is a catch: they must feed each other the sundae using spoons which have been taped to the end of broom handles! This activity can lead into a discussion about how Christians have to help each other in discipleship. (However, it can also lead to spoon-related injuries, so please take care!)

Ideas for All Age Worship

Set up a whiteboard or pin board as people enter the worship space, and ask them to share on it their 'top tips for discipleship'. It might be daily prayer habits, good books they have read or devotional resources they have used, or any other ways in which your congregation remind themselves and encourage themselves to keep following Jesus.

If the young people have done the Psalm 23 activity from 'Going Deeper' then they may want to share this with the wider congregation. It may be good to have the whole congregation read the Psalm responsively, so that it becomes part of the whole congregation's worship and not a performance.

You might want to ask people to think about role models.
Can people think of three spiritual role models: one from the Bible, one from history/culture and one who is a person in their every day life?
Perhaps two or three people would be willing to share with the wider congregation about what role models they have chosen and why?

About the Authors

H. C. Dill
Henna is a freelance writer and Christian youth worker. She lives in Aberdeenshire, Scotland with her husband and two children. Dill holds both a First Class Honours Degree and a Masters-by-Research in Theology from the University of Aberdeen. She has many years of experience in children and youth ministry, working with groups of all shapes and sizes, across different denominations.
To contact H. C. Dill, and to be kept up-to-date on future publications in this series, please visit the author's social media pages on Facebook (H.C.DillWrite) or Instagram (@h.c.dill.write).

M. McKinnell
Mary has an interest in Ignatian Spirituality, and much of her writing comes out of using spiritual practices from this tradition. She draws on scripture and on a wide variety of personal and church related experiences for inspiration. An active Christian, with many years' experience working for the church as a communications mission officer, Mary enjoys helping others to communicate Christ's love to the local community.
She is also a trained spiritual director and enjoys this ministry, listening to others and supporting them in their relationship with God.
Mary is available to lead worship services, reflective days and residential retreats to help people of all ages to spend time with God. You can view more of Mary's work or contact her via her blog: searchingforunderstanding.com

Printed in Great Britain
by Amazon

57041725R00047